THIS
NOTEBOOK
BELONGS TO

Made in the USA
Monee, IL
15 January 2022

89026331R00069